Poster Pack

Cute, fun, and inspiring posters from American Girl!

★ AmericanGirl®

Dear Reader,

Add a touch of style to your space—just tear out and hang a poster from this pack. Wallpaper your room with precious pets and adorable dolls. Line your locker with sweet sayings that are sure to brighten the gloomiest day. And don't forget to share the perfect poster with a special friend!

Your friends at American Girl

Published by American Girl Publishing, Inc.
Copyright © 2010 by American Girl, LLC

Questions or comments? Call 1-800-845-0005,
visit our Web site at **americangirl.com**,
or write to Customer Service, American Girl, 8400 Fairway Place, Middleton, WI 53562-0497.

Printed in China
10 11 12 13 14 15 16 17 LEO 10 9 8 7 6 5 4 3 2 1

All American Girl marks are trademarks of American Girl, LLC.

Editorial Development: Carrie Anton

Design: Chris David, Lisa Wilber

Production: Jeannette Bailey, Judith Lary, Sarah Boecher, Tami Kepler

Create!

All things grow with **love.**

I can do anything

Owl always be your friend.

★ American Girl®

Laugh!

Try Something New!

American Girl®

Think positive!

Peace!

Imagine

American Girl

Hop
to
it!

What I think matters!

Drop
on
in!

✪ American Girl®

Express yourself!

★ American Girl®

American Girl®

Have a heart!

You'll go
farther
with a
friend!

Reach
for the
stars!

★ American Girl®

GO for it!

★ AmericanGirl®

I can be
strong.

A hug makes everything better.

BEE A TEAM PLAYER!

American Girl®

BLOOM

SMILE

★ American Girl®

Find a way to **brighten** each day.

Keep your eye on the ball!

American Girl®

Smile :)

American Girl®

Lazy Days

★ American Girl®

Find your inner strength!

Just hangin' out!

⭐ American Girl®

Express

yourself!

Happy tails to you!

★ American Girl®

Celebrate
you!

relax

I'm fawned of you!

The road to a friend's house is never long.

What posters are in your room? Write to:
Poster Pack Editor
American Girl
8400 Fairway Place
Middleton, WI 53562

(All comments and suggestions received by American Girl may be used without compensation or acknowledgment. Sorry—photos can't be returned.)

Photo: © istockphoto/vusta

Here are some other American Girl books you might like:

❑ I read it.

❑ I read it.

❑ I read it.

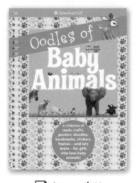
❑ I read it.

❑ I read it.

❑ I read it.